Old Art of Tea

There is a legend about how people were inspired to take advantage of the tea plant in the first place. About 4,000 or 5,000 years ago, Shen Nong was the patriarch of a tribe in prehistoric China, who possessed the power to bring timely rain and make the sun emit enough light and heat. His other accomplishments included collecting crop seeds and teaching people how to grow them. At that time, the earth was ravaged by pestilence, and people contracted diseases and died in multitudes. In order to find a medicine to fight the plague, Shen Nong tasted all kinds of herbs and plants. So, tea was discovered by chance.

Legend has it that one day Shen Nong tasted 72 poisonous herbs, and was poisoned as a result; it was the leaves of a tea tree he inadvertently picked and tried that saved his life. Although some people are skeptical about this legend, derived from the *Shen Nong Compendium of Materia Medica* (*Shen Nong Bencao Jing*), it makes sense that primitive man, who lived mainly by hunting and gathering, should have found by accident the therapeutic function of tea leaves while they were collecting and trying plants for food.

Shen Nong Compendium of Materia Medica (*Shen Nong Bencao Jing*).

Shen Nong tasting herbs.

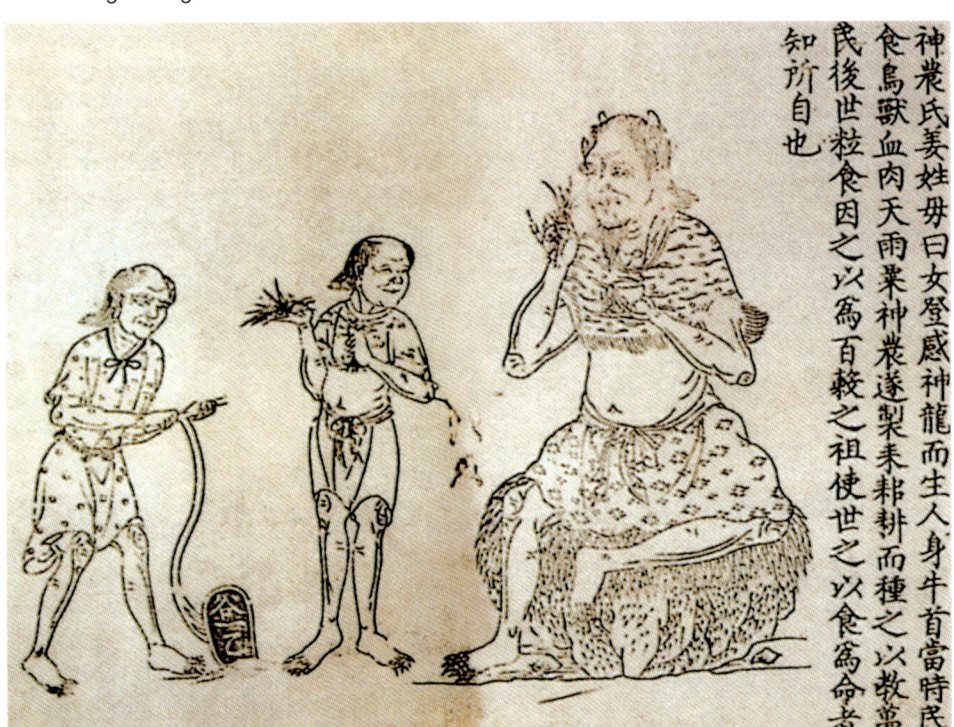

Before the Qin Dynasty (221-207 BC), tea drinking was a practice mainly limited to the areas of Ba and Shu, two vassal states of the Zhou Dynasty (c.11th century-256 BC). The two states covered nearly the same territory as today's Sichuan Province and Chongqing Municipality. The earliest regional annals in China, *The Annals of Huayang State*. *The Annals of Ba*, says, "King Wu of Zhou (the first ruler of the Zhou Dynasty) overthrew the last king of the Shang Dynasty with soldiers from Ba and Shu.... Having conquered Yin (another name for the Shang Dynasty), King Wu allowed the people of Ba to bear the surname of the ruling house, and granted their leader the title of viscount.... Red paint, tea and honey ... were sent as tribute." These words indicate that as early as some 3,000 years ago, tea was already being cultivated in the ancient Ba and Shu areas, and used as tribute paid to the Zhou kings in the Central Plains.

紵魚鹽銅鐵丹漆茶蜜靈龜巨犀山雞白雉黃潤鮮
粉皆納貢之其果實之珍者樹有荔支蔓有辛蒟園
有芳蒻香茗給客橙葵其藥物之興者有巴戟天椒
竹木之瑨者有桃支靈壽其名山有塗籍靈臺石書
邢山其民質直好義土風敦厚有先民之流故其詩
曰川崖惟平其稼多黍旨酒嘉穀可以養父野惟阜
丘彼稷多有嘉穀旨酒可以養母其祭祀之詩曰惟
儀惟澤蒸命良辰祖考來格其好古樂道之詩曰惟
月孟春獺祭彼崖永言孝思享祀孔嘉彼黍既潔彼
月明明亦惟其名誰能長生不朽難獲又曰惟德實

A page from *The Annals of Huayang State. The Annals of Ba*, a book by Chang Qu of the Eastern Jin Dynasty (317-420), with records of tea growing in the State of Ba.

The Ba and Shu areas played a significant role in the early development of the tea industry after the Qin Dynasty (221-206 BC) unified China. In the succeeding Han Dynasty (206 BC-220 AD), these areas were the most important consumer market for tea, and the largest base where tea was gathered and distributed. In 59 BC, Wang Bao from Zizhong, Sichuan, wrote in rhymed prose: "An Agreement with My Servant" (*Tong Yue*). In it, he stipulates that his servant should "make tea with proper utensils, and purchase tea in Wuyang." Wuyang is today's Pengshan County, Sichuan. This indicates that there already existed tea markets in Sichuan in the Han Dynasty, and that tea drinking was a common practice in the Ba and Shu areas. Before the Tang Dynasty (618-907), the Chinese word for tea, *cha*, possessed many aliases, including *tu* and *ming*. It was in the middle of the Tang Dynasty that the word *cha* first came into use. When Lu Yu wrote *The Classic of Tea* (*Cha Jing*) in the year 780, he changed all the words *tu* into *cha*, and listed *tu* as an alias for *cha*. Since then, *cha* has been accepted as the orthodox word for tea, and the meaning, writing and pronunciation of the word established at that time are still in use today.

Portrait of Wang Bao.

"An Agreement with My Servant" (*Tong Yue*) by Wang Bao, Western Han.

The earliest method of drinking tea was to put the newly plucked leaves of wild tea plants directly into a pot to boil. Guo Pu of the Eastern Jin Dynasty (317-420) mentioned in the annotation he made to the *Er Ya*, the earliest Chinese dictionary, compiled between 221 BC and 220 AD: "The tree is as small as a gardenia. The leaves, which grow even in the winter, can be boiled and drunk as soup." During the Three Kingdoms Period (220-265), Zhang Ji wrote in his *Guang Ya* (a book on textual exegesis): "People in Jing and Ba collect tea leaves, and make them into the shape of cakes. The tea cakes are cooked together with rice paste." This is the earliest record of tea processing in China. At that time, freshly plucked tea leaves were compressed into cakes. When people felt like drinking tea, these tea cakes were roasted until they turned red, pounded into powder, and then put into a porcelain vessel. Boiling water was subsequently added, along with some Chinese onion and ginger, to produce a mixed beverage. The custom of tea drinking spread northward as cultural communication between the north and the south dramatically increased during the Western and Eastern Jin dynasties (265-420) and the Southern and Northern Dynasties period (420-589). In fact, it was during these periods that today's tea-producing areas along the middle and lower reaches of the Yangtze River started to take shape.

But tea was not as popular in the Central Plains as it was in the south at that time. It was people from leading families of scholar-politicians in the south who took a most sincere delight in tea. Lu Na of Eastern Jin was one of the tea addicts. When he served as governor of Wuxing, he once served General Xie An of the State of Wei, only tea and dried fruit. That is where the saying "Serving good, incorrupt officials with tea" is derived. Wang Meng, a native of Jinyang in today's Taiyuan, Shanxi Province, who lived during the early stage of the Eastern Jin Dynasty, was one of the rare tea lovers among the northern aristocrats. At that time, many members of the northern nobility had emigrated to the south. Wang never failed to treat them with abundant tea every time they called at his house. The northerners, however, were unimpressed by this "watery stuff."

The Tang Dynasty was one of the most open and powerful dynasties in Chinese history. With vastly improved communications in the newly re-unified nation, tea production and distribution flourished. Tea spread from the south to the Central Plains, from the Central Plains to the ethnic-minority regions along the borders, and on to Korea and Japan. In the later part of the dynasty, tea became a "beverage of the whole nation."

Porcelain kettle used for brewing tea leaves during the Han Dynasty. Pictured is a funerary object, several sizes smaller than the real thing.

A bronze cauldron, also Han Dynasty, into which tea would be poured, and Chinese onion, ginger and other ingredients added.

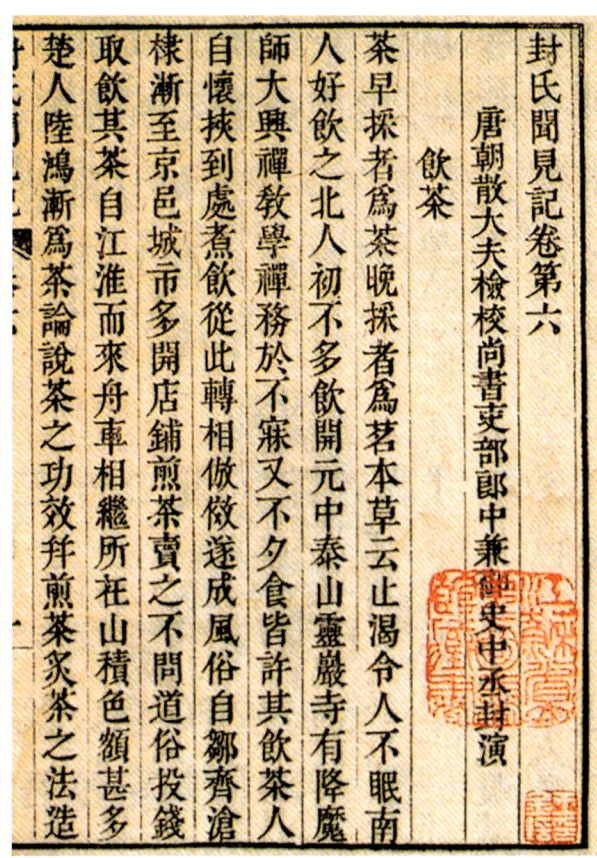

Things Heard and Seen by Feng (*Fengshi Wenjian Ji*), by Feng Yan, Tang Dynasty.

The flourishing of Chan Buddhism in the Tang Dynasty stimulated a wider acceptance of tea. Feng Yan, a Tang scholar, wrote in his *Things Heard and Seen by Feng* (*Fengshi Jianwen Lu*): "In the middle of the Kaiyuan Period (713-742), a master exorcist devoted himself to the promotion of Chan at the Lingyan Temple on Mount Taishan. He studied Chan doctrine day and night without sleeping, eating nothing in the evening and only drinking tea. People learned about this, and speculated that there must be something extraordinary about tea. Many set about boiling and drinking tea. Thus it became a custom."

Tea-producing areas grew more extensive in the Tang Dynasty. The plant was cultivated in 43 prefectures and sub-prefectures scattered in the eight major tea habitats of Shannan, Huainan, Zhexi, Jiannan, Zhedong, Qianzhong, Jiangnan and Lingnan in southern china. In Changxing County, Zhejiang Province, an area was set aside to produce tea for the exclusive use of the imperial court. The first of its kind in Chinese history, the base grew and processed one of the most famous teas at that time: Guzhu Purple Bamboo Shoots. As the tea industry continued to grow, the government began to tax the product, and tea taxes thenceforth became an important source of revenue for the following dynasties. Under the reign of Tang Emperor Suzong (756-762), the government started to exchange tea for horses with the Huihu (ancient name for the Uygur people of northwest China). This trade continued into the Song Dynasty (960-1279).

Portrait of Emperor Dezong (780-805) of the Tang Dynasty. Because the government treasury was almost depleted after the An Lushan-Shi Siming Rebellion, Emperor Dezong started to levy a tax on tea on the advice of Zhao Zan, Vice-Minister of Revenue. This was the beginning of the tea tax in China.

A ruined teahouse on the ancient Tea and Horse Caravan Trail, dating from the Tang Dynasty, in Fengqing, Yunnan Province.

"Since Lu Yu came into the world, people have vied with each other to learn how to make fresh tea." These two lines of a poem remind us that no history of China's tea culture is complete without mentioning Lu Yu (733-804), who influenced posterity in a most profound way by exalting tea drinking to a lofty cultural and artistic activity. Lu was from Tianmen, in central China's Hubei Province. Despite the hard life in his early years, he devoted most of his life to studying how tea should be cultivated, processed, prepared and drunk. He summarized the experiences of his precursors and wrote the first monograph on tea in the world, *The Classic of Tea*. Venerated as the "god of tea" and the "saint of tea" by posterity, Lu laid a solid foundation for tea study in the coming years by his systematic theory of tea-related science and culture.

The Classic of Tea consists of three volumes and ten chapters: Chapter One, *Origin*, describes the physical qualities and features of tea, the ideal environment for tea plants' growth, and the natural functions of tea; Chapter Two, *Instruments*, introduces the instruments for picking and processing tea; Chapter Three, *Production*, gives the best time for picking tea leaves, the standards for selecting tea and the methods of processing it; Chapter Four, *Utensils*, lists tea wares used for preparing and drinking tea designed by Lu himself, and their functions; Chapter Five, *Preparation*, describes how to prepare tea; Chapter Six, *Drinking Tea*, discusses his investigation into the history of tea drinking, and explains the methods of tea drinking in his day; Chapter Seven, *Stories*, relates legends and anecdotes about tea from prehistoric times to the Tang Dynasty; Chapter Eight, *Sources of Tea*, introduces the eight major tea-producing areas in the Tang Dynasty; Chapter Nine, *Simplification*, introduces some simplified ways of processing and preparing tea, and some simplified instruments for doing so; and Chapter Ten, *Diagrams*, records the contents of the whole book in diagrams, which serve as a guide for the entire process of producing, brewing and drinking tea.

The most common tea in Tang times was that made into the shape of cakes, called "tea cakes." Seven steps were required to produce a tea cake — plucking, steaming, pounding, patting, roasting, piercing and sealing. The job involved first putting the newly harvested leaves in a steamer to steam, then pounding the leaves into paste while they were still hot. The paste was poured into molds after that, and patted into the shape of cakes. The next step was to roast the tea cakes over a fire, followed by using a thin strip of bamboo bark to pierce the dried tea cakes from the center to hold them together. Then the tea cakes were sealed and stored.

Making tea with tea cakes demanded particular care. One first had to roast the cakes to get them dehydrated, then crush them into powder with a grinder, sieve the powder, and finally put the sieved powder into a cauldron to boil.

As well as tea cakes, there also existed coarse tea (*cu cha*), loose-leaf tea (*san cha*) and powdered tea (*mo cha*) in the Tang Dynasty, the different methods of drinking them being elaborated in *The Classic of Tea*.

10

Palatial Pleasure (detail), Tang Dynasty. The painting depicts a tea ceremony held by a group of court ladies.

Xiao Yi Obtaining the Orchid Pavilion (detail), believed to have been painted by Yan Liben, Tang Dynasty. The painting shows two domestic servants, one old, one young, preparing tea.

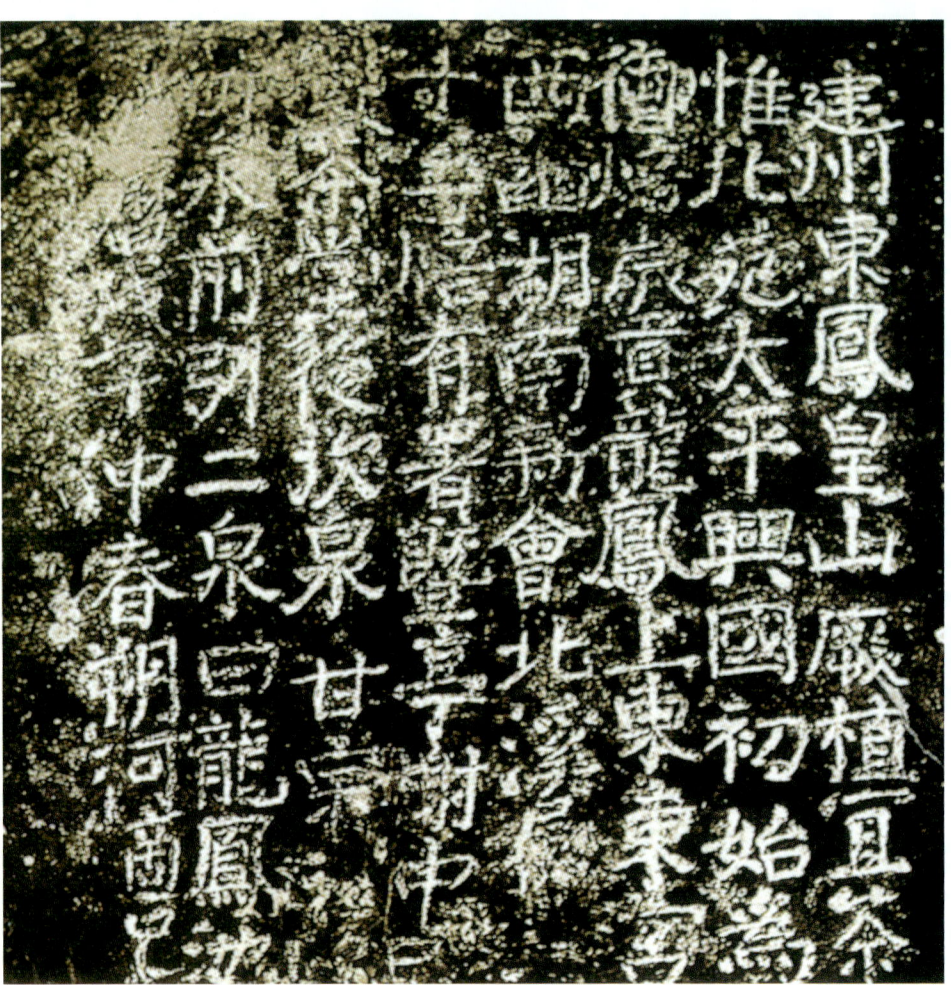

Rubbing of one of the cliff carvings found in the ancient Beiyuan
Tea Plantation on Phoenix Mountain, Jian'ou, Fujian Province.

On the basis of the development of the tea industry in Tang times, the Song Dynasty (960-1279) saw the scale of manufacture enlarged. The processing techniques grew more sophisticated, and there emerged Dragon and Phoenix Tea Cakes, which later became prized luxury items. The center of tea trading shifted southward, to northern Fujian in southeast China. The base where tea was produced for imperial use also moved, from Guzhu to Jian'ou, Fujian Province. Loose-leaf tea, which first appeared in the Tang Dynasty, kept gaining popularity among ordinary people, and teahouses mushroomed. "Tea competitions," became universally popular during the Song Dynasty.

Portrait of Cai Xiang (1012-1067). A famous calligrapher of the Northern Song Dynasty, Cai was obsessed with tea culture throughout his life. While serving as the official in charge of public finance and goods transportation of Fujian, he for some time supervised the Beiyuan Tea Plantation, which sent tea as tribute to the imperial court. Cai was the author of *A Record of Tea* (*Cha Lu*), in which he elaborated on the tea preparation method of his day known as *dian cha*, and the tea wares involved.

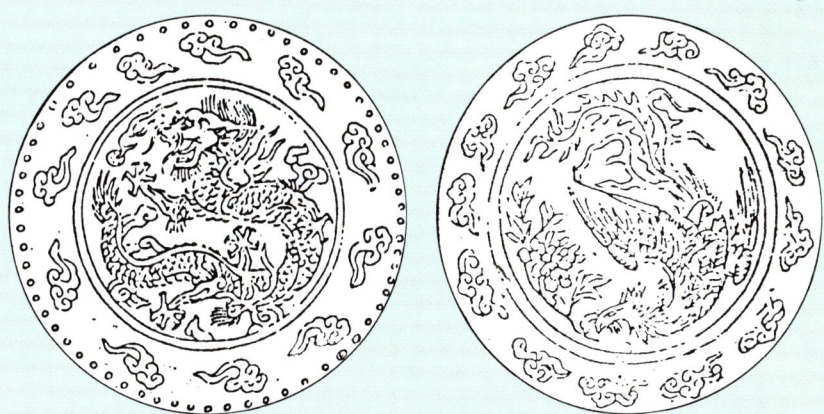

Patterns of Dragon and Phoenix Tea Cakes. A famous product of the Beiyuan Tea Plantation in Jian'ou, Dragon and Phoenix Tea Cakes were made in a very exquisite fashion, with dragon and phoenix designs pressed into the surfaces from molds. Many variations were available, each with a different name.

14

Tea Competition (detail), Song Dynasty.

"Tea competitions" date back to the Five Dynasties (907-960), originating somewhere around Jian'an, Fujian Province. Because of Song Dynasty Emperor Huizong's passion for the game and the participation of many of the literati, the pastime soon became a fad across the country. Many literary works of that time mention the game, of which the most famous is Fan Zhongyan's *Reply to Zhang Ming's Tea Competition Ode*. Generally speaking, there were two types of tea competition. One was mainly pursued by people of the upper classes — the members of the imperial court and the aristocrats — who laid down strict criteria, ranging from the selection of tea cakes to the specific procedures of the game. The other was mostly practiced by the lower classes, who took delight in the technical aspects of the game and the sheer pleasure of participation. A vivid scene of such a competition held by a group of town folks can be seen in the painting *Tea Competition* by Zhao Mengfu, a prominent painter of the following Yuan Dynasty (1206-1368). The procedure went like this: First, the tea-cups were heated with hot water. Then "the paste was concocted," i.e., a certain amount of tea powder was put into the cups according to their sizes. A little cold water was mixed with the tea powder. Then, boiling water was poured into the cups. While the hot water was being poured in, the contestant had to keep stirring the tea vigorously with a tea whisk, so as to produce a layer of white froth on the surface of the tea. The color of the foam was one of the two subjects of the competition; the other was to see if the froth could "bite the cup" (*yao*

15

Portrait of Zhao Ji, Emperor Huizong (1082-1135) of the Song Dynasty. Huizong took delight in tea drinking, and wrote *A Study of Tea in the Daguan Period* (*Daguan Cha Lun*), i.e., during his reign.

Literary Gathering (detail), by Zhao Ji. A group of literati are enjoying tea. *Dian cha* or "whisking tea," the way of preparing tea popular at the time is illustrated in detail in the lowest part of the painting.

zhan), which is to say, whether the froth covered the surface of the tea completely. A nicely done job had very white froth that stayed for a long time and "bit the cup." Foam of clumsily brewed tea, which dispersed quickly, was described as "disappearing like clouds' feet" (*yun jiao san*). The fashion for tea competitions, at its height in the Song period, began to fade in the Yuan Dynasty, and almost entirely vanished in the Ming Dynasty (1368-1644).

Dian cha, was developed in the Song Dynasty from the *jian cha* (boiling tea) method of the Tang Dynasty. The procedure included grinding Dragon and Phoenix Tea Cakes into powder with a tea grinder, sieving the powder, putting the sieved powder directly into tea cups and pouring in boiling water while stirring the brew with a tea whisk

The mural painting inside a Liao Dynasty tomb in Xuanhua, Hebei Province, reflects the tea drinking custom of the dynasty.

so as to produce a layer of froth above the tea.

The tea industry was boosted during the Song Dynasty particularly by the need to procure horses for the constant wars with Song's northern neighbors. Tea was in great demand among the nomads of the western regions, and a regular caravan trade grew up to purchase horses for tea.

Steps on the ancient Tea and Horse Caravan Trail in Pu'er, Yunnan Province. Tea from Yunnan and Sichuan was carried by horse caravans to be exchanged for horses in Tibet. The tea-horse trade flourished in the ethnic minority regions from the Tang Dynasty to the Qing Dynasty (1644-1911).

17

Site of the ancient Tea-Horse Trading Office (*Cha Ma Si*) on Mount Mingshan, Sichuan Province. The office was in charge of the business of exchanging tea for horses from the Tang Dynasty to the Qing Dynasty.

18

A mural painting found in Benzilan, Deqen County, Yunnan Province, showing a horse caravan returning home.

Portrait of Zhu Yuanzhang, or Emperor Taizu of the Ming Dynasty.

In 1391 or the 24th year of his reign, Zhu Yuanzhang, or Emperor Taizu of the Ming Dynasty, decided that making tea cakes was too time-consuming. Besides, tea lost much of its natural flavor after being made into tea cakes. So he decreed that tea cakes be abolished, and loose-leaf tea used instead. After that, loose-leaf tea gradually replaced tea cakes, and the two leading methods of preparing tea popular in the Tang and Song dynasties, *jian cha* and *dian cha*, were replaced by the method of simply pouring boiling water on the loose leaves.

The fact that loose-leaf tea finally triumphed made the appearance of a variety of famous teas possible. Tea leaves were processed with much more attention paid to the outer look and inner quality of the tea. Various methods of tea processing were worked out through experiments. The consequence was the emergence of a diversified array of processed teas, such as scented tea (flower tea), black tea, red tea and green tea.

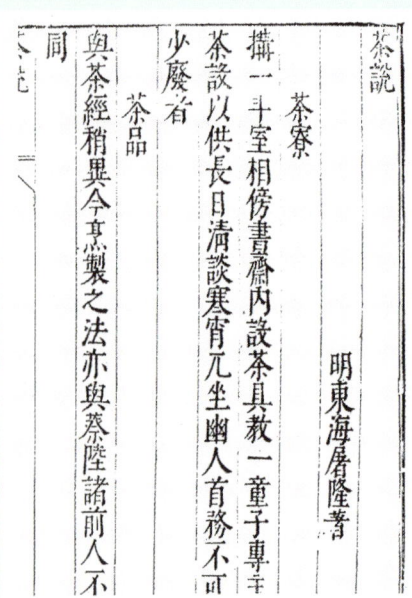

On Tea (*Cha Shuo*), by Tu Long, Ming Dynasty.

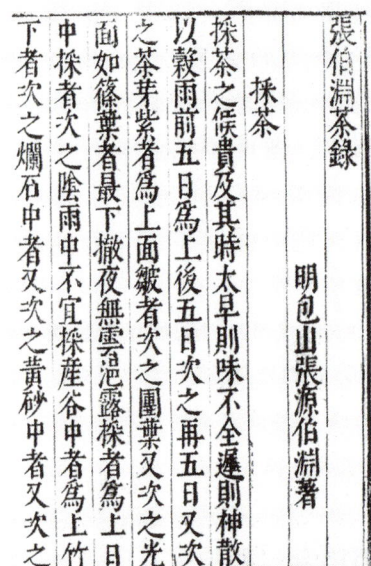

A Record of Tea (*Cha Lu*), by Zhang Yuan, Ming Dynasty.

Rubbing of *Seven Tips on Brewing Tea* (*Jian Cha Qi Lei*), by Xu Wei (1521-1593). Xu was a prominent Ming Dynasty calligrapher, painter and writer.

Another important contribution to China's tea culture made during the Ming Dynasty was the great amount of scholarly research on tea. *The Encyclopedia of Tea* (*Chaye Quanshu*) by Wan Guoding says that more than 50 kinds of books focusing on tea were published during the dynasty, almost half the number of books about tea published from the Tang Dynasty to the Qing Dynasty. The literary elite of the Ming Dynasty cherished an intimate emotional bond with tea. The practice of making tea not with tea cakes but with tea leaves,

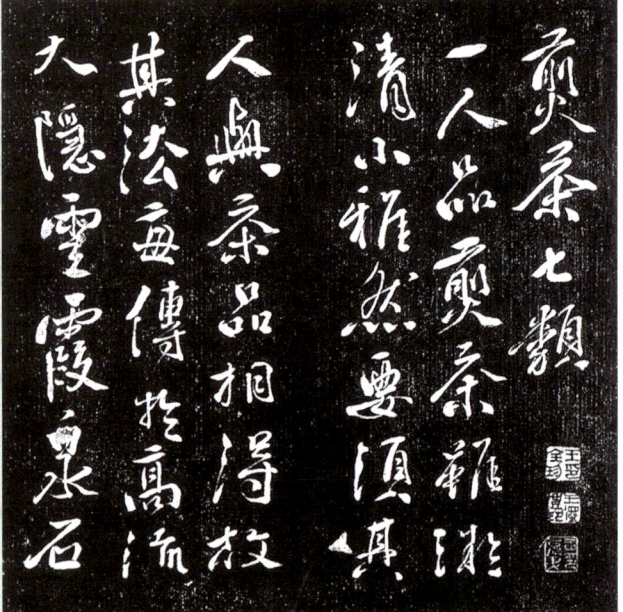

which laid more emphasis on tea's true nature, was in harmony with late Ming intellectuals' pursuit of returning to Nature and seeking a true and simple spiritual world. Writers and poets of the age were inspired to produce memorable literary works, while many painters chose to express their attachment to the lifestyle embodied by tea-drinking through painting.

This painting commemorates the occasion on the Festival of Pure Brightness in the 13th year (1518) of the Zhengde reign period, when Wen Zhengming (1470-1559) and two friends held a tea party on Mount Hengshan, near Wuxi. Nicknamed "The Hermit of Mount Hengshan," Wen was one of the representative painters of the Wumen School of the Ming Dynasty.

The tea industry continued to prosper throughout the Qing Dynasty (1644-1911). Both the tea-growing areas and the annual output of the product increased greatly, and tea exports reached historic highs in the middle and late periods of the dynasty. The booming domestic and overseas markets provided merchants from Anhui, Shanxi and Guangdong with a grand stage to perform on, and many a trader made a fortune out of tea. Tea stores and teahouses sprang up all over China, as tea culture became a regular part of the people's daily life. The tea industry had entered a new era of commercialization.

Tea stacked for export from Shanghai Port in the late Qing Dynasty.

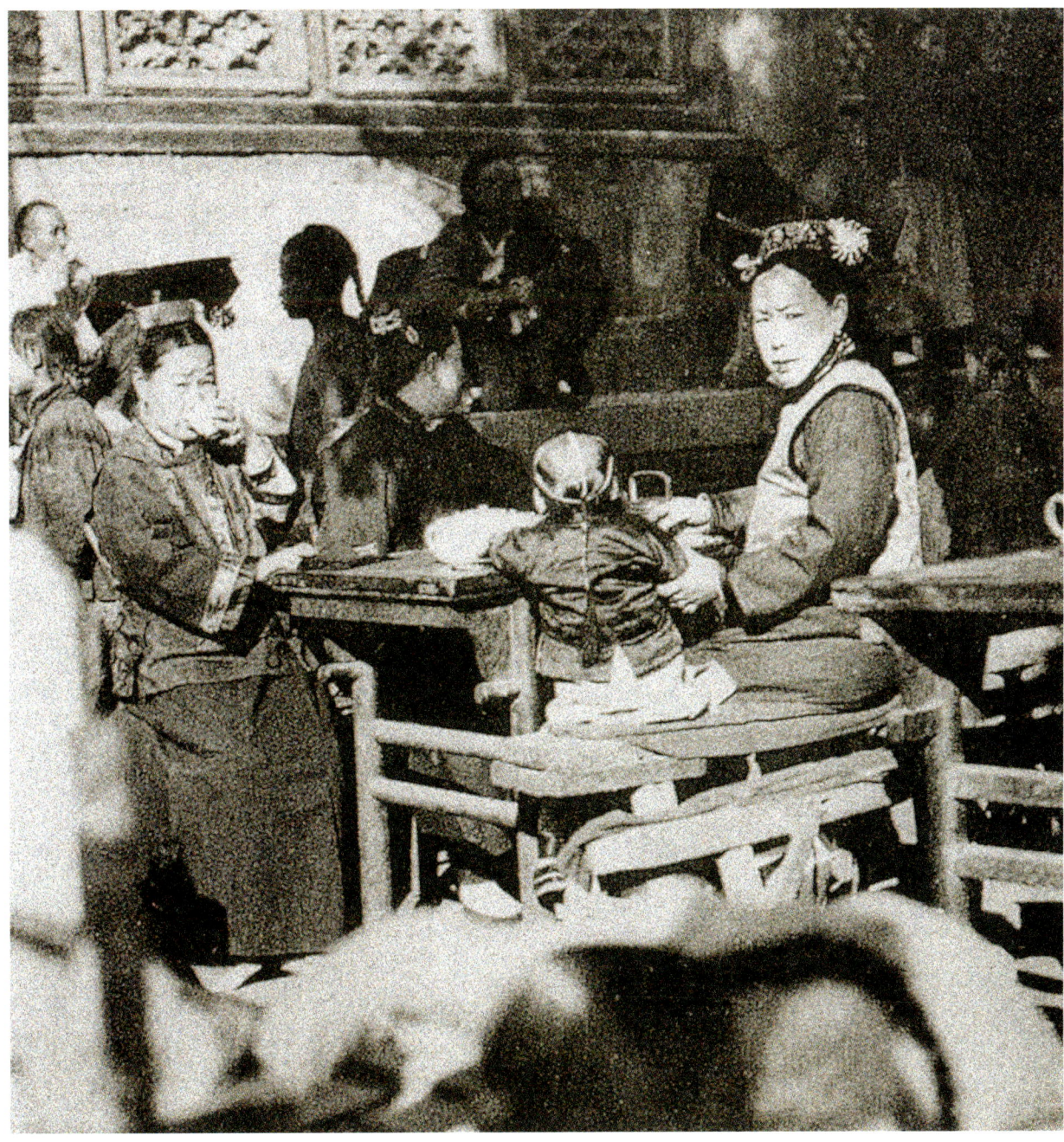

A Qing Dynasty Beijing teahouse.

Stamps printed with pictures of tea porters. Published in 1894 and 1897 by the Hankou (Hankow) Post Office. The stamps give us a clue about the importance of the tea trade in China at that time.

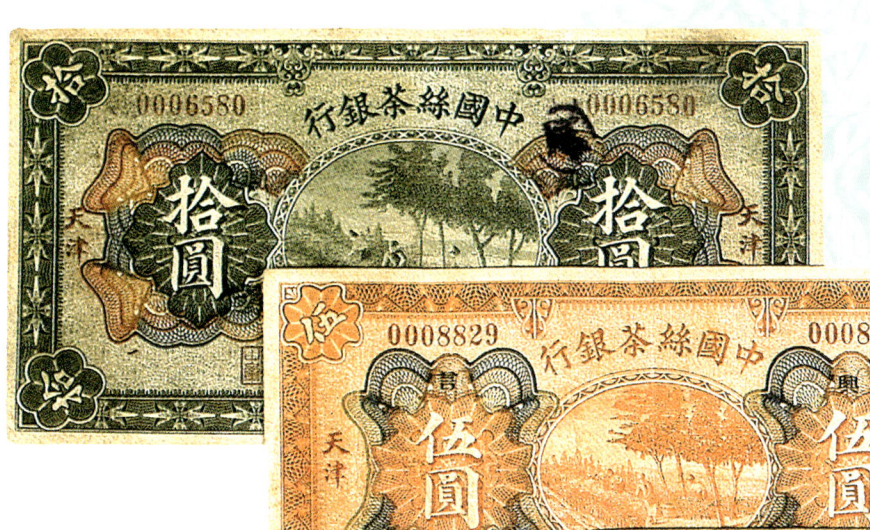

Notes issued by the Silk and Tea Bank of China. A commercial bank aimed at boosting the development of the tea and silk industries, the bank's notes mainly circulated in north China.

Famous Chinese Teas

China's long history and expansive area for tea cultivation have given rise to numerous tea plant species, and Chinese tea growers and producers have accumulated an abundance of experience over a prolonged course of experimentation. The dazzling assortment of tea varieties emerging as a result always impresses people by their ingenious processing techniques, fine quality and exquisite flavors.

Tea Cultivation

It took a long time for the ancient Chinese to progress from gathering tea leaves in the wild to the first attempt of grow tea plants themselves. According to the *Tong Jun Lu* written in the late Eastern Han Dynasty, there were already five or six tea-producing areas in China. Wu Lizhen, a man of the preceding Western Han Dynasty, was said to have "planted eight divine tea bushes" on Mount Mengshan, Sichuan, and was regarded as the first person to manage to cultivate tea in China.

The site where Wu Lizhen, the forefather of China's tea cultivation, was said to have "planted eight divine tea bushes" on Shangqing Peak, Mount Mengshan, Sichuan in the Western Han Dynasty (206 BC-25 AD).

Lu Yu of the Tang Dynasty wrote in *The Classic of Tea*: "As far as soil is concerned, the best (tea) grows among mushy rock, mediocre gritty soil, and the worst yellow earth." The most desirable soil for tea plants' growth, Lu believed, is "mushy rock," by which he meant soil produced by weathered Paleozoic rock, sandstone and slate. Modern science holds that acidic soil, red or yellow in color, and with a pH between 4.5 and 6.5, renders the most beneficial soil conditions for the growth of tea bushes.

Fertilizing Young Tea Plants, painting produced for export, Qing Dynasty.

Asexual propagation by tip cuttings in modern tea plantations.

Asexual propagation of tea plants.

Tea was grown directly from individual seeds in the Tang Dynasty, but in the Ming Dynasty people started to sow several tea seeds together in one hole, and then raise tea plants by transplanting the mature clusters of shoots. This technique, known as layerage, was first used in tea cultivation in Fujian Province, but exactly when it was initiated is not known. Today, tea farms are managed following the requirements of modern science, including choosing a beneficial ecological environment, planning the use of the land, constructing drainage and irrigation systems and facilities to prevent soil erosion, planting windbreaks and sun-screening trees, plowing the soil, choosing tea plant species, sowing the seeds or raising cuttings and then transplanting them, and using the close-planting strategy as appropriate.

Tea Picking

The words "hewing and picking," which appear in *The Classic of Tea* indicate that in the early days of tea cultivation people might have climbed up the tea trees and chopped off the tips of the branches. As tea plants in certain southern areas are trees of rather tall stature, some locals trained monkeys to pick tea leaves for them. Nowadays, tea leaves can be picked by machine; nevertheless, hand-picking is still preferred in many places, as it is felt that this is the only way to meet the special tea-picking requirement for preserving the traditional varieties of tea.

31

Monkeys picking tea leaves.

Picking tea leaves on an early 20th-century Chinese tea plantation.

Tea-picking methods vary by regions and seasons. According to the periods when the shoots start and stop growing, tea is defined as spring tea, summer tea, autumn tea, and even winter tea (which is only possible in southeastern China). Tea is also categorized as "first flush," "second flush," and "third flush" during the growing season. The time span in a year during which tea can be harvested varies depending on the climate. Tea can be harvested for at least five to six months a year in the area south of the lower reaches of the Yangtze River, seven to eight months in southwest China, nine to ten months in certain areas in south China, and almost throughout the year in Hainan Province.

Picking tea leaves on a modern tea plantation in southern China.

Tea Varieties

The Chinese people originally chewed fresh tea leaves to prepare tea for drinking. Later, they boiled them in water. This was followed by steaming and compacting the leaves into tea cakes. Finally, the pan-frying method was adopted.

Tea is generally divided into two groups, according to the processing method and quality: basic tea and reprocessed tea.

There are six types of basic tea — green tea, red tea, oolong tea (also called by the Chinese "*qing cha*," or green tea, because of its greenish-brown color), yellow tea, white tea and black tea.

34

Green Tea

Green tea is the dominant variety in China, being produced in 19 tea-growing provinces and autonomous regions. China supplies 70 percent of the green tea traded on world markets.

Characterized by "clear liquid and green leaves," green tea is made through a procedure including *shaqing* (meaning "killing the green") in which the newly picked leaves are heated to a high temperature for a short time to kill the oxidizing enzymes, kneading and rolling (so as to squeeze out extra moisture and release the flavor enzymes from the leaves), and finally drying out. There are four ways of doing this — pan-frying, roasting, sun-drying and steaming.

The prepared leaves of three types of green tea (top to bottom): Xihu Long Jing (West Lake Dragon Well), Huangshan Mao Feng, and Zhu Cha (Bead Tea).

The translucent luster of West Lake Dragon Well tea.

Pan-fried green tea:

Making for a large part of China's green tea product, the tea is made going through a course involving *shaqing*, kneading and rolling, and pan-frying to get the leaves dry. By shape it can be defined as long pan-fried green tea, round pan-fried green tea, and flat pan-fried green tea.

Roasted green tea:

Freshly picked leaves are heated under high temperature to prevent oxidization, pressed and rolled, and roasted to go dry. The finished tea presents an attractive appearance with the whole slender string of each leaf undamaged during the processing and the white pekoe on it still visible. The dark green tea leaves, somehow oily, assume a tender and bright color after being steeped, and deliver a liquor with fresh fragrance and mellow flavor. Depending on the degree of the tenderness of leaves and the techniques used for processing, this category can be divided into ordinary roasted green tea and tender roasted green tea.

35

Tea leaves being pan-fried to make green tea in the 19th century.

Tea leaves being pan-fried during the processing of *Mingqian Long Jing* (Pre-Pure Brightness Festival Dragon Well tea).

Sun-dried green tea:

Dried by sunlight, it is chiefly used for compressed tea like *tuo cha*, *jin cha*, tea cakes, square tea and *kang zhuan*, and is mainly produced in Yunnan, Sichuan, Guizhou, Guangxi, Hubei and Shaanxi.

Steamed green tea:

The freshly picked leaves are steamed to stop the activity of oxidizing enzymes. They are then carefully kneaded and rolled before being allowed to dry. The tea is known for the attractive green color of the processed tea leaves and the liquid, and the way the leaves unfurl in the water.

Red Tea

Fresh leaves are left to wither for a certain period after they are picked, and then twisted and rolled in order to crack the surface so as to release the oxidizing enzymes. Then the oxidization or fermentation process begins. The green leaves are left to completely oxidize till they turn reddish-copper. A final drying takes place. This tea is called "red tea" in China, and "black tea" in the rest of the world. Today, red tea tops other teas in terms of global output and sales. By processing method and quality, China's red tea can be sorted into kungfu red tea (*Gong fu hong cha*), small-species red tea (*Xiao zhong hong cha*) and small-pellet red tea (*Hong sui cha*).

Kungfu red tea:

This tea derives its name from the painstaking processing method, which involves many subtleties in the shape, color, aroma and flavor of the tea. Quality products demand that every single leaf be curled and twisted tight, undamaged, and of the same size, the color of the leaves lustrous black and the brew bright limpid red. The liquid features a full and pure fragrance and a rich, mellow flavor with a hint of sweetness. The major producing provinces are Anhui, Yunnan, Fujian, Hubei, Hunan and Sichuan.

Small-species red tea:

A special product of Fujian, this tea differs from kungfu red tea most conspicuously in the fact that it is dried over an open fire of pine wood, thereby obtaining an intense pine-smoke aroma.

Small-pellet red tea:

Developed from kungfu red tea in the late 19th century, this tea has the appearance of small and tightly pressed pellets, with a black color that sometimes takes a brown tint. This tea produces a dark-red liquid with full-bodied freshness, ideal for the addition of sugar, milk or lemon.

Red teas (from top to bottom): *Qihong* (Qimen red tea), *Dianhong* (Yunnan red tea) and *Xiao zhong hong cha* (small-species red tea).

The dark appearance of small-species red tea.

Oolong Tea

A semi-fermented tea something halfway between unfermented green tea and fully fermented red tea, oolong tea is sometimes referred to by the Chinese as "*qing cha*," or green tea, because of its greenish-brown hue. This tea is mainly produced in three provinces: Fujian, Guangdong and Taiwan. A typical oolong tea leaf is green in the middle and red on the edges, and so Chinese people often describe it as a "green leaf with a red rim." Steeping oolong tea yields a golden bright liquid that has a mellow flavor and a long aftertaste.

Oolong tea: *Tie Guan Yin.*

Yellow Tea

This tea gets the distinctive yellow color of both its leaves and the liquid it produces from the unique processing step of piling the leaves thickly for a certain period in order to force a yellow color on them. The tea gives out a pleasant refreshing aroma, and has a mellow and thick flavor. By size and degree of tenderness of the buds or leaves used as raw material, the tea is usually sorted into "yellow bud," "small yellow tea," or "big yellow tea."

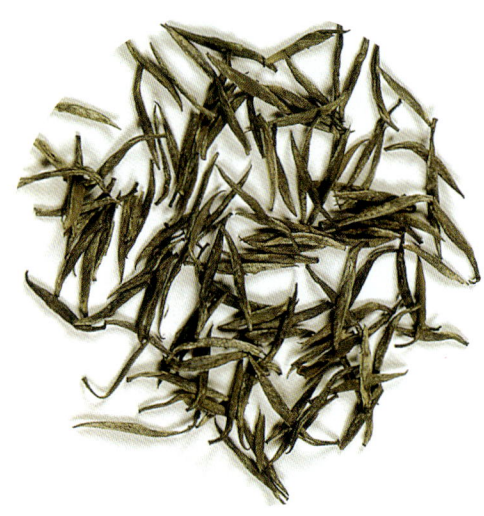

Yellow tea: *Junshan Yin Zhen* (Mount Junshan Silver Needle).

40

White Tea

Chiefly a Fujian Province specialty, this is a slightly fermented tea, going through such processing steps as sun-drying or oven-drying. White tea is often made of leaves mantled by a layer of white fuzz, hence the name. The finished tea leaves have a delicate, silvery white appearance due to the original white pekoe. Steeping yields a faint-colored liquid with a fresh and mellow flavor. By the material used, white tea is classified as "bud tea" and "leaf tea."

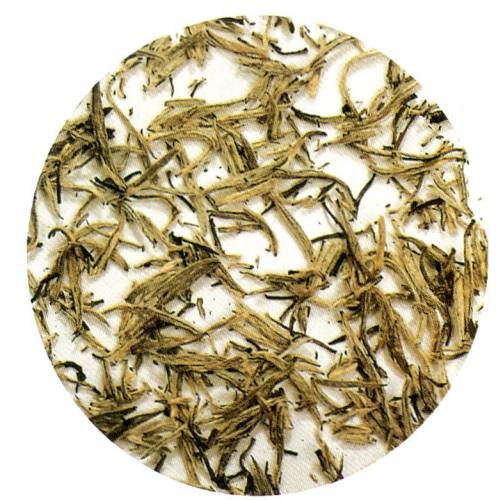

White tea: *Bai Hao Yin Zhen* (Silver Needle with White Pekoe).

Black Tea

This is a post-fermented variety peculiar to China, its processing involving *sha qing*, kneading and rolling, piling up and drying. The finished leaves exhibit a heavy and oily black color, which turn brown in a bright yellow liquid after being steeped. Black tea is mainly produced in Hubei, Hunan, Sichuan, Yunnan and Guangxi, and mostly sold in ethnic-minority regions such as Tibet, Qinghai and Xinjiang.

41

Black tea: Pu'er tea.

The appearance of freshly brewed Pu'er tea.

Reprocessed Tea

Reprocessed tea is any of the above-mentioned six teas being further processed in a certain way. The leaves are mixed with fragrant flowers so as to absorb the flowers' scent, compressed into cakes, squeezed to extract desired substances from the leaves, or blended with fruit juice. Accordingly, reprocessed tea can be defined as scented tea, compressed tea, extracted tea, and dietary tea.

Scented tea:

Scented tea is produced mainly in Fujian, Jiangsu, Zhejiang, Anhui, Sichuan and Guangdong provinces. The tea is made by mixing the leaves of green tea or red tea with certain aromatic flowers. People living in the northern areas of China are quite fond of drinking scented tea, which pleases with a delicate flower scent mingled with the tea's original flavor. Scented tea has a lot of varieties. According to the scent the tea absorbs, it is divided into jasmine tea, amara tea, rose tea, gardenia tea, and so on.

Scented tea: jasmine tea.

The appearance of freshly brewed jasmine tea.

Compressed teas: (Above) *sunke cha* (Bamboo Shoot Sheath tea) of the Guangxi Zhuang Autonomous Region; (Below) *tuo cha* (Tuo tea) of Chongqing Municipality.

Compressed tea:

Compressed tea is usually made from black tea by steaming, compressing into different shapes, and drying. Compressed tea is mainly sold in the ethnic-minority areas in the northwest and southwest of China. Famous varieties in this category are *tuo cha*, *Pu'er cha*, *Liubao cha*, black brick tea and *Xiang jian cha*.

Compressed teas: (Left) *zhutong xiangcha* (Bamboo Tube Scented tea) of Yunnan Province; (Right) *Anhua hua zhuan* (Anhua Flowery Brick tea) of Hunan Province.

43

A demonstration of tea etiquette by the West Lake.

The Art of Brewing Tea

The Chinese are finicky when it comes to preparing tea, regarding it as nothing short of an art to brew a cup of tea with a fine color, aroma and flavor. After thousands of years of experience with tea, they have turned the activity of serving and enjoying their everyday cup of tea into an art of daily life.

The environment in which the tea is served is another aspect the ancient Chinese, especially the classic and elegant types, attached great importance to. Tea appreciation used to be held in a carefully selected environment, preferably a place surrounded by natural scenery to lend people a poetic mood.

The West Lake Dragon Well.

The Lushan Spring reputed ▶
by the Chinese as "The First
Spring under Heaven" on
Mount Lushan.

Discussing Painting Beside Songxi Brook, by Qiu Ying, Ming Dynasty.
Two scholars are engaged in a quiet but inspiring discussion on painting,
leisurely sitting by a brook and accompanied by the sound of the wind
wafting through pine tree branches. A young servant is scooping water
from the brook; another is attending a boiling kettle on a stove. The picture
reflects traditional Chinese intellectuals' preoccupation with a tea-drinking
environment that satisfies both the eyes and the mind.

How to Brew Tea in a Scientific Way

The Chinese attach great importance to water for a good brew. Since ancient times, "The tea of Longjing (Dragon Well) and the water of Hupao (Tiger Running Spring)," and "The water from the midstream of the Yangtze River and the tea from the top of Mount Mengshan" have been regarded as the best pairs for making tea. It is generally believed that "water is the mother of tea," and that it takes the incorporation of the right leaves and the right water to fully bring out the potential flavor of tea.

The second rule is that tea wares are also of great importance to the quality of tea. Different teas should go with different types of tea wares. People generally tend to steep green tea in glasses, oolong tea in kungfu tea vessels, and red tea in purple clay pots. The utensil called *gaiwan*, literally "lidded bowl," is what the northern Chinese prefer when it comes to steeping scented tea.

One must first be equipped with an understanding of the characteristics of all types of tea. The inherent character of tea will be able to be fully released if scientific methods are applied. In general, the three most important things one should bear in mind are the proportion of leaves to water, the water temperature and the period of steeping.

The proportion of leaves to water:

Generally speaking, water should be added to dried leaves of red tea or green tea in a proportion of about 1:50, namely, for three grams of dried leaves, about 150 grams of water should be added. Brewing oolong tea requires more leaves, with the proportion of dried leaves to water at about 1:25. Of course, the proportion is adjustable so that a stronger or weaker liquid will be made according to one's desire.

The water temperature:

High-grade green tea should be steeped in water at a temperature of about 80 degrees Celsius, which will guarantee a liquid with a bright green color and a lively refreshing flavor. Water at too high a temperature will spoil the tender leaves by making them overdone and turning them yellowish. Ordinary green tea, red tea and scented tea, are better steeped at a water temperature just below boiling. Oolong tea and Pu'er tea, which have relatively large and coarse leaves, should be steeped in 100-degree-Celsius boiling water.

Generally speaking, tea is best served with not more than three infusions. This is because usually the first infusion releases 50 percent of the soluble compounds from inside the leaves, and the second one releases about 30 percent. Therefore, when it goes on to the third infusion, there is less than 20 percent of soluble substance left to be retrieved.

The period of steeping:

After being steeped in boiling water, tea leaves first give out substances like caffeine, vitamins and amino acids. The content of these substances in the tea will reach the peak value in three minutes, and as a result bring forth the tea's best flavor around that time. Three minutes later, as the content of solubles like tea polyphenols increases in the water, a somewhat astringent quality will be accumulated in the tea.

Brewing Green Tea

Green tea is best served in a colorless glass. Place three grams of premium-grade green tea leaves in the glass, and pour in 80-degree-Celsius water, first to only a fourth of the desired amount. Allow the leaves to steep for some 20 to 40 seconds, so that they unfurl little by little and the inner substances slowly seep out. After that, lift the teapot high above the glass, and pour more water into it three times. The leaves will then swirl up in the current, and through the transparent glass one will be able to see the leaves suspended in the water, sinking and dancing in a graceful manner. Then, green tea with airy freshness is ready to drink.

A demonstration of tea etiquette .

Brewing Oolong Tea

Oolong tea is usually prepared with kungfu tea ware originating in the Fujian area, where people daily practice the traditional art of "kungfu tea." A set of kungfu tea ware includes several articles each with a classical name: "Yushu wei" is a pottery kettle; "Mengchen guan" is a purple clay pot believed to have been invented by Hui Mengchen, a famous purple clay craftsman, hence the name; "Ruochen ou" indicates a set of four white porcelain teacups; and "Chaoshan lu" refers to a small stove.

The brewing process starts with the rinsing of the teacups with hot water. They are then placed on a tray. A generous amount of leaves is put into the teapot until they fill more than half of the pot. Boiling water is then poured over the leaves from a kettle that is raised high above the teapot, until the water overflows the mouth of the teapot. The foam floating on the liquid is scraped away by the lid of the teapot before the lid is replaced. After that, hot water is sprinkled onto the lid so as to help the brewing, which is finished in a short while, and the tea is ready to be served. The host then fills the teacups in a fashion that manages to let the tea in each cup be of the same strength, and completely empties the teapot. In Hong Kong and Taiwan, kungfu tea ware even includes a "scent-smelling cup," with which a tea taster will first smell the scent of the tea before going on to take the first sip. At that point, a delicate fragrance will permeate both the nose and mouth, and saliva will naturally arise. Indeed, kungfu tea is a sensuous pleasure that should be relished very carefully.

1

2

3

Brewing Oolong tea (Top to bottom): Arranging the tea set; rinsing the cups; warming the teapot; adding the tea leaves; infusing the leaves; removing the foam; adding more water; filling the cups (a process known as "Lord Guan inspecting the guards"); making sure that the last drop is poured (called "Han Xin's muster roll").

4

7

5

8

6

9

Brewing Red Tea

As the most widely consumed tea in the world, red tea has a mild character. This tea can be drunk by itself or mixed with other ingredients, depending on one's preference.

When drunk by itself, red tea is prepared by first cleaning the tea ware, then putting a certain amount of tea leaves into a teapot with a teaspoon, and finally pouring in boiling water at about 90 degrees Celsius from a kettle lifted high above the teapot at a proportion of 50 to 60 ml of water to one gram of dried leaves.

Red tea can also be enjoyed with milk, lemon, sugar, etc., which is quite popular outside China.

1
3
2
4

Brewing red tea: 1. Rinse the teapot and the teacup with hot water; 2. Put the leaves into the teapot with a teaspoon; 3. Pour boiling water into the teapot, and replace the lid. Allow the leaves to steep for two to four minutes; 4. Place a strainer on the cup, pour into the cup the brewed liquid through the strainer, and remove the strainer containing filtered tea leaves. The tea is now ready to drink.

Tea Wares Through the Ages

As an embodiment of the art of tea drinking and serving, and a witness of the development of China's tea culture, tea wares have evolved from coarse to refined, from complex to simple, and from rich antique ornamentation to artless elegance.

"Tea depends on water, and water depends on instruments." Xu Cishu of the Ming Dynasty thus described what instruments meant to tea in his *Cha Shu* (*Comments on Tea*). In the broader sense, tea instruments include devices used in all tea-related activities ranging from picking, processing, storing and preparing to drinking. The articles involved include tea baker, container, boiler, grinder, and utensils used to prepare and drink tea. The last group is what we commonly refer to as "tea ware." Tea wares come in the forms of pottery and porcelain, tin, bronze, jade, lacquer, and glazed items. The most widely produced and used are made of pottery and porcelain.

Tea Wares with Multiple Functions

In the early development of China's tea culture, tea ware was often used for the purposes of eating and drinking alcohol as well.

In the Eastern Jin and Southern Dynasties periods, when tea was mainly popular in south China, tea ware mainly consisted of a bowl and a *bo* (an earthenware article in the form of a small basin).

56

Pottery jar with stamped ornamentation, Warring States Period (475-221 BC).

Celadon bowl with a lotus petal design, Southern Dynasties period (420-589).

Tang Tea Wares

Tea became a national beverage from the mid-Tang Dynasty, with tea wares manufactured in large quantities by porcelain kilns in both the north and the south of China. The style of the age was summarized as "celadon in the south and white in the north," represented respectively by the porcelain of the Yue Kiln, which featured glaze representations of towering green mountains, and that of the Xing Kiln, famous for its silvery and snowy glaze. Aside from these two top-notch kilns, the kilns in Changsha, Shouzhou, Hongzhou and Yuezhou were also prolific tea ware producers. Tea ware at that time mainly consisted of bowls, saucers, *zhuzi* or ewers, and tea grinders. A Yue Kiln tea bowl and a pitcher were excavated from a Tang tomb in Xi'an, giving as a good idea of the style of tea ware in those days.

Celadon bowl made at the Yue Kiln, Tang Dynasty (618-907).

White-glazed bowl made at the Xing Kiln, Tang Dynasty.

Celadon cup made at the Yue Kiln, Five Dynasties period (907-960).

Apart from pottery and porcelain tea wares, Tang craftsmen also made tea utensils out of gold, silver and other materials. A set of tea wares once used by the imperial court was unearthed in Fufeng County, Shaanxi Province. These objects, the most luxurious so far discovered, were made of expensive materials such as gold, silver and glaze, and included a tea container, tea warmer, tea grinder, salt container, charcoal tongs and poker, tea pots and cups.

Gilded silver tea container with depictions of flying geese, Tang Dynasty.

Gilded tea grinder, Tang Dynasty.

Gilded silver salt container with a design of Makaras, Tang Dynasty.

Gilded tea sieve, with a design of celestial deities riding cranes on its walls, Tang Dynasty.

Gilded silver tea spoon, Tang Dynasty.

Song and Yuan Tea Wares

In the Song Dynasty the *dian cha* (whisking tea) method of tea preparation came into vogue, displacing the *jian cha* (boiling tea) method popular during the preceding Tang Dynasty. A Song tea art expert prepared tea with 12 special items, including a tea stove, tea mortar, tea grinder, tea sieve, tea whisk, tea saucer, teacup, *tang ping* and tea towel. Among them, the *tang ping*, meaning "soup bottle," was the most important utensil for *dian cha*. Song boasted an advanced and thriving porcelain industry, with tea wares produced in all five of its most renowned porcelain kilns — the Ru Kiln, Guan Kiln, Ge Kiln, Ding Kiln and Jun Kiln. "Tea competitions" were a national craze during the Song Dynasty, and black-glazed cups were highly prized, because they provided the best contrast with the pale-colored tea. These cups were manufactured in large numbers both in the Jian and Jizhou kilns in the south, and the Cizhou and Yaozhou kilns in the north. A mural in the Guangsheng Temple, Hongtong County, Shanxi Province, although it dates from the Yuan Dynasty (1206-1368), shows details of tea preparation very much in the Song style.

Picture of tea wares drawn in the Song Dynasty (960-1279).

Longquan celadon bowl, Song Dynasty.

Black-glazed cup with partridge design, made at the Ding Kiln, Song Dynasty.

Black-glazed cup with rabbit-hair-like cracks, made at the Jian Kiln, Song Dynasty.

Lotus-shaped glass cup and saucer, Yuan Dynasty.

Detail of a Yuan Dynasty mural in the Guangsheng Temple, Hongtong County, Shanxi Province. On the lower right maid-servants are preparing tea.

Ming Tea Wares

In the Ming Dynasty (960-1279), the method of pouring boiling water directly on loose-leaf tea replaced both the *dian cha* and *jian cha* fashions. This resulted in new features of tea ware. The black-glazed cups popular in the Song Dynasty were replaced by ones of white porcelain, *qing hua* (porcelain with underglaze cobalt-blue designs) and colored porcelain. Jingdezhen emerged as the porcelain-producing center of the country in this period. Zhang Yuan, a Ming scholar, remarked in his *A Record of Tea* (*Cha Lu*): "Cups snowy white in color are superior." Tea set with matching teapot and cups became fashionable during the Ming Dynasty, a trend which continues today. Another feature of Ming tea utensils was the popularity of Yixing purple clay tea ware, which was prized because it helped to retain the original flavor of the tea and keep the leaves from going stale, and was a better heat insulator. The age yielded many master purple clay pot craftsmen, including Shi Dabin, Li Zhongfang and Xu Youquan.

Porcelain bowl with cobalt-blue underglaze, Ming Dynasty.

Purple clay pot unearthed from a tomb dating from the 12th year (1533) of the Jiajing reign period.

Porcelain bowl with cobalt-blue underglaze and a curling dragon design, Ming Dynasty.

Qing Tea Wares

The method of tea preparation and the tea wares used in the Qing Dynasty (1644-1911) did not differ much from those of Ming times. Jingdezhen still represented the highest quality of porcelain, and produced a large number of tea wares created both for the exclusive use of the imperial court and for the general market. Qing porcelain makers developed a richer diversity of glaze than those of the previous dynasties. Apart from cobalt-blue underglaze and glazes in many other colors, it also yielded much more ornate categories such as famille rose and enamel glaze.

Qing tea wares, varied in form and shape, were mainly composed of *gaiwan* (lidded bowl), tea saucer, tea tray, tea canister and teapot case. *Gaiwan*, also called *juzhong*, is made up of a lid, a bowl and a base. The lid was added for the purpose of keeping the heat in and the dust out. The base was added so that the drinker could hold the hot bowl more comfortably. Steeping tea in *gaiwan* was typical of Qing times. It was the most commonly used utensil whether serving tea for guests at home or in teahouses. Qing saucers came in many variations. One was called a "tea boat" because of its two upturned ends (bottom, page 66).

Chrysanthemum-shaped purple clay pot with green ground and red glaze, painted with gilt decorations, Qianlong reign period (1736-1796).

A household teapot container.

The Qing period saw more varieties of purple clay tea ware than the Ming period. Among them, purple clay ware with overglaze painting prevalent in the middle part of the dynasty was a hybrid of purple clay craftsmanship and Jingdezhen overglaze technology. Hand-made works by Qing purple clay masters like Chen Mingyuan, Chen Mansheng and Yang Pengnian were much sought after by collectors at that time.

Famille rose lidded bowl painted with melons and butterflies, Qing Dynasty.

Color-glazed saucer.

Color-glazed "tea boats."

Purple clay pot with a grape design, Qing Dynasty.

Modern Tea Wares

Ever-evolving modern technology promises more possibilities for the ancient art of tea ware making. With an increasing number of accomplished artists showing an interest in this field, more and more new-style tea wares with original concepts and specific themes are appearing.

Modern tea ware.

Modern bamboo-carved tea ware.

The China National Tea Museum in
Hangzhou, Zhejiang Province.

A corner of the exhibition hall of the China National Tea Museum.

Tea Etiquette and Ethnic Minorities' Tea Customs

As China's long history of tea culture unfolded, different tea-related customs took root among different ethnic groups in China living in different historical periods and in different social milieus. A nation of etiquette, the Chinese have traditionally used tea to make guests feel welcome. The old saying "three cups of tea when a guest comes" used to be generally observed: The first was to show respect; the second to start the conversation; and when the third cup of tea was served — and the tea had gone rather insipid — the guest got the signal to leave.

Tea-Related Wedding Customs

Tea is symbolic of the quality of being pure and firm, and is regarded as a wish to have many children. People like to cite sayings such as "Tea isn't easy to contaminate" to indicate pure love; "A transplanted tea tree cannot live any more" to endorse constant love; and "many saplings under a tea tree" to symbolize the happiness of having many children. In many Chinese wedding customs taking shape over the centuries, tea has played an important cultural role.

In ancient China, when a marriage was agreed between two families, betrothal gifts sent by the groom's family to that of the bride always included tea, and so the act of sending the gift was called *xia cha*, or "laying down the tea," and the wedding was called *shou cha*, or "accepting the tea." In the areas south of the lower reaches of the Yangtze River, there used to be a custom called the "three teas and six gifts." The "three teas" included *xia cha* on the occasion of engagement, *ding cha* (fixing the tea) at the wedding, and *he cha* (combining the teas) on the bridal night. In some places, the teas served respectively at the proposal, the young man and the young woman's first formal meeting, and the bridal night were called the "three teas."

Ethnic Minorities' Tea Customs

Tea holds an important place in many ethnic minority people's life. The rich and colorful tea customs developed and observed by different ethnic groups are part of China's valuable cultural heritage.

Tibetan Buttered Tea

The Tibetans love to drink buttered tea. Tea drinking helps reduce body fat accumulated as their diet comprises a good deal of meat and cheese. Tea also provides the vitamins they otherwise would lack, as they live on a plateau with limited access to vegetables. As a result, the Tibetans are known for "rather spending a day without meat than without tea."

Tibetan buttered tea is made like this: Boil crushed brick tea or *tuo cha* (a bowl-shaped compressed mass of tea leaves) in a kettle. Pour the boiled tea into a pot, and mix it with butter, sesame powder, peanut kernels, melon seed kernels, pine nut kernels and salt. Keep stirring the brew with a wooden stick until the tea, butter and the other seasonings are completely blended. Pour the brew into a kettle to be heated for a few minutes. This produces a slightly salty, oily and robust-flavored tea.

73

Making Tibetan buttered tea.

Mongolian Milk Tea

Tea also holds an important place in the Mongolian people's daily life, especially nutritious and sustaining milk tea. The Mongolians usually prepare milk tea early in the morning, and keep warming it up over a small fire all day.

To make Mongolian milk tea, first boil crushed brick tea in water in an iron pot or kettle. After the liquid turns reddish brown (in about ten minutes), boiled cow's or sheep's milk, along with a little salt, is added. Stir the brew well, and the result is a hot, heartily-flavored beverage. The Mongolians are well known for their hospitality. When a guest arrives at the yurt of a Mongolian family, the host will first present him, using both hands, with a large plate of dairy products, such as cheese, milk curd and butter. Then milk tea will be served, which the guest should accept with both hands. He should then move the tea to his left hand, dip the tip of the third finger of his right hand in the tea, toss it up in the air, and lick the fingertip. This is meant to show his gratitude for the host's hospitality. Milk tea is an indispensable part of the Mongolians' daily life.

A Mongolian yurt.

Drinking milk tea while listening to the *matou qin* (Mongolian musical instrument with a horse-head decoration).

Mongolian tea wares.

Tujia Pounded Tea

The Tujia people live in the border area between Sichuan, Guizhou, Hunan and Hubei provinces, where China's tea trees originated. Intimately connected with the plant, the Tujia have a special tea called *lei cha*, or pounded tea, with which they treat guests. Because the beverage is made by boiling raw tea leaves, raw ginger and raw rice together in water, it is also called *san sheng cha* — literally, "three-raw tea."

To make pounded tea, first put tea leaves into a mortar along with seasonings such as soybeans, green beans, peanuts, sugar and sesame. Then slowly pound them into a paste with a wooden pestle, and add cold water and mix it all together. The pounded tea's sweet and delicious flavor is good for quenching thirst and appeasing hunger.

Materials used to make pounded tea.

Dai Bamboo Tube Tea

Called *naduo* in the Dai language, bamboo tube tea is offered to guests of the Dai people living in Yunnan Province, southwest China. A handful of fresh tender tea leaves is placed in a tube of the *xiang zhu* (fragrant bamboo) species, and roasted over an open charcoal fire. When the leaves shrink, a wooden stick is poked into the tube to press them tight, and new leaves are put in. This is repeated until there is no room in the tube for more leaves. When the roasting is finished, the tube is split open, and the tea leaves are retrieved. The host then breaks off a piece of tea from the tea column, puts it in a bowl, instills in boiling water from the brass kettle, brew it for a while and serve to the guests. The tea has a fresh aroma of bamboo.

Making bamboo tube tea.

Bai Three-Course Tea

This peculiar fashion of serving tea is reserved for guests by the Bai people who live around the picturesque Mount Cangshan and Erhai Lake in Yunnan Province. The first course consists of tea made with green tea leaves that have been roasted in an earthen pot. The tea, with robust flavor, tastes a little bitter. The second course is brewed after adding brown sugar and a dairy product called "milk fan" to the tea, which give a full sweetness to the liquid. When it comes to the third course, honey, walnut kernels, sliced ginger and Chinese prickly ash seeds are added, giving the tea a complicated and pungent aftertaste. The carefully arranged sequence of the different tastes of the three courses of tea, "first bitter, then sweet, and finally a meaningful aftertaste," as the locals put it, is full of symbolic meaning.

Three-course tea of the Bai people.

Jino Cold Tea

The Jino people mostly live on Mount Jinuo in Jinghong County, in the Xishuangbanna Dai Autonomous Prefecture, Yunnan Province. The Jino ethnic group have a long history of growing tea, and their habitat is a famous tea producer. The local specialty — Pu'er tea — is well known both in and outside China.

The Jino make cold tea with fresh tender tea leaves and also eat the tea leaves as food. It is tasty, and easy to make. First, rub the newly picked tender leaves hard between the hands, and put the crushed tea leaves in a bowl. Add pulverized orange tree leaves, pepper, salt and garlic. Finally, add some spring water, stir with chopsticks, and put it aside for about 15 minutes before tasting. The brew is cool, salty and spicy. It is also nutritious and refreshing. Cold tea can be said to be an early example of taking tea leaves as food.

A Jino woman making "cold tea."

Lahu Baked Tea

The Lahu ethnic group live mostly in the areas of Lancang, Menglian, Cangyuan, Gengma and Menghai in Yunnan Province. Drinking baked tea is an old tradition of the Lahu people, and still popular today.

The baked tea, also called "pop hot tea" or "*lazhaduo*" in the Lahu language, is very easy to make: Bake newly picked tea leaves over a fire until they turn brown. Then put them in a tea pot, and pour in boiling water. After a short while, the tea is ready to be drunk.

Baked tea looks clear yet a bit yellowish, with a somewhat roasted fragrance, mellow yet slightly bitter and sour. It has the function of quenching the thirst and stimulating the appetite. Drinking it often will invigorate one's spirits. To this day, the Lahu people use baked tea as a medicine.

The theater attached to the Huguang Guild Hall in Beijing. Visitors appreciate Chinese culture while watching performances of traditional operas over a cup of tea.

Chinese Teahouses

Teahouses have long been an intimate part of the Chinese people's life, and indeed are an interesting and distinctive cultural phenomenon. Though now it is hard to tell exactly when they originated, one thing is for sure, and that is they were the result of the popularity of tea drinking.

It is generally believed that in the Tang Dynasty, the tea peddlers who carried two buckets of tea dangling from a shoulder pole and wandered about the streets, and the mobile tea booths in the cities were the precursors of teahouses. Teahouses burgeoned in the Song Dynasty. In the famous painting scroll, *Festival of Pure Brightness on the River* by the Northern Song (960-1127) painter Zhang Zeduan, teahouses are dotted along the river flowing through the capital. Teahouses were also often the venues for performances of Yuan opera and *ping tan* (storytelling in the local dialect combined with ballad singing) during the Yuan Dynasty. Thus emerged the tradition of Chinese teahouses hosting small-scale theatrical performances. In the Ming and Qing dynasties, teahouses took on more diversified forms and a more expansive range of functions.

Festival of Pure Brightness on the River (detail), by Zhang Zeduan, Northern Song. Teahouses are shown in abundance in the painting.

和尚治遊

佛自周昭王時下生迄於滅度
足誌未嘗履中國王
和尚朝東說乃後八百年而有
漢明帝託談姹夢志
出遊湯事乘今之傳人偏天
下失異寔邪令吳
佛門弟子但棄顯行不法久亦
不于源覽事乃前日
本譯老丹惟戲圖夜演時東
一和尚手操聰扁耳服
羅裙高坐正應妄談時事詞
天咳到一妓競堂異音
以遊以婚相很相得權以魏態
不可詣舉夫原其此
家之記某父母生而不能賣寫
而樂河婦亦不駁歷畫
顛姿獻應篤雜玄頭玄期
清泥大本煎身記臣
業道入堂門道跡銷聲視
克忘兜横未有告邪本
生如此情恩注探妄呈
行如此之初為甚虽
人妖如已矢有司宜雄印
訪查置揭站詣中
以著羅急而昭烱歲

Places meant for giving people a chance to quench their thirst and to taste a good beverage originally, teahouses have deviated from their original simple orientation as urban society has evolved. They have become an important socio-cultural arena, welcoming people from all walks of life. With no need to hurry, no social status to worry about, only a cup of tea in hand — which wipes out the social distance between the tea drinkers — people have comfortably turned teahouses into miniatures of society.

87

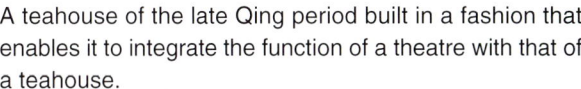

A teahouse of the late Qing period built in a fashion that enables it to integrate the function of a theatre with that of a teahouse.

A playbill advertising performances taking place in certain Tianjin and Beijing teahouses in the early part of the 20th century.

A tea store on Nanjing Road, Shanghai, in the late Qing Dynasty.

Fang Lu Ge, a teahouse typical of those in the area south of the lower reaches of the Yangtze River, located in Wuzhen, Zhejiang Province.

Gaiwan cha (lidded-bowl tea), a specialty of Chengdu, Sichuan Province.

Teahouses in different parts of China exhibit very different features due to the country's vast territory and the varied tea-drinking customs. Almost all of them are endowed with typical local flavor. The most representative of them can be found in Beijing, Guangzhou, Chengdu and the areas south of the lower reaches of the Yangtze River.

New-style "tea-art houses" have given city dwellers another leisure alternative in recent years. With their serene inner space, they offer people a quiet place to rest their minds and hearts from time to time in the midst of bustling city life.

The interior of the Men'er Tea-Art House in Hangzhou, Zhejiang Province.

Teahouse by Hangzhou's scenic West Lake.

A modern Taiwan teahouse.

93

The Spread of Tea around the World

As the birthplace of tea, China introduced to the rest of the world directly or indirectly the *camellia sinensis* species through cultural exchanges. Today, people in more than 160 countries and regions drink tea, and the number of countries and regions that grow tea has increased to over 50, with the total world output surpassing 3,020,000 tons a year. The most important tea-producing countries are China, India, Sri Lanka, Indonesia, and Kenya, among which Sri Lanka claims the most exports — more than 280,000 tons in 2000; China was next with an estimated 230,000 tons exported in that year. Nowadays, each person consumes an average of half a kg of tea annually worldwide.

A modem Japanese tea plantation.

Chinese tea was exported as early as during the Southern and Northern Dynasties, when China exported tea leaves to the Turks in exchange for other goods. The Tang Dynasty witnessed a booming overseas trade in tea, which was carried all the way along the Silk Road through the Huihe region and the states in the Western Regions (areas covering today's Xinjiang Uygur Autonomous Region and parts of Central Asia) to Western Asia and the Arab countries. Tea leaves, tea wares and tea-preparation methods reached Korea along with the expansion of Buddhism to the Korean Peninsula from China. It is generally believed that tea started to be grown in Korea in the late years of Tang Emperor Taizong's reign (627-650), when Silla envoy Daeryeon took back the seeds of tea plants from China and planted them at Hwaeom Temple at the foot of Mount Jiri. Today, Korean tea etiquette still bears some traces of Tang culture.

Guoqing Temple on Mount Tiantai, first built during the Sui Dynasty (581-618).

It is believed that from as early as the Kaihuang reign period (581-600) of the Sui Dynasty Japanese monks had begun to come to China to study Buddhism, and they took back with them Chinese tea culture, as well as the doctrines of Buddhism. Two prominent Japanese Buddhist monks, Saicho and Kukai, are given the credit of first cultivating tea plants in Japan. In 804, Saicho came to study Buddhism at Guoqing Temple on Mount Tiantai, Zhejiang Province. He took back some seeds of tea plants with him, and planted them in Shiga Prefecture, Japan. Kukai studied Tantric mysticism in the Tang capital Chang'an (modern Xi'an). He took back with him not only the seeds of tea plants, but also the technique for processing tea. In the Song Dynasty, the Japanese monk Eisai, who twice studied Buddhism in China, wrote *Drink Tea and Stay Healthy*, the first monograph on tea in Japanese history. The book laid the foundation for Japan's tea ceremony, or *chado*.

The oldest tea plantation in Japan.

Portrait of Eisai. The prominent Japanese Buddhist monk came to China to study Buddhism in 1182, and took back with him techniques for growing and processing tea, and tea wares. He was the author of *Drink Tea and Stay Healthy*.

The Memorial Hall to Kukai. The Japanese Buddhist monk came to study Tantric mysticism at the Qinglong Temple, Chang'an in 804, or the 20th year of the Zhenyuan reign period of the Tang Dynasty. He took Chinese tea seeds and tea wares home with him.

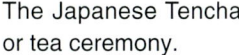

The Japanese Tencha, or tea ceremony.

Sri Lanka's tea estate.

In the Ming Dynasty, the great explorer Zheng He commanded fleets of ships on seven voyages, traveling far across the oceans. His journeys led him to Vietnam, Java, India, Sri Lanka, Arabia, and as far as the east coast of Africa. Along the route of Zheng's voyages Chinese tea flowed to South Asia and on to Africa. As early as in the 14th century, tea had already been introduced to Morocco, one of today's largest consumer countries of Chinese green tea.

The Malaysian tea-making procedure known as teh tarik.

Europe first greeted tea in 1609, when the Dutch imported it from China and Japan through Java. One of the countries that launched the European tea trade was Portugal, which imported Chinese tea in great quantities in its trading ships. The English convention of taking tea is said to have been introduced by Princess Catherine of Braganza of Portugal, whose enthusiasm for the beverage was shared by other members of the English royal family after she married the king of England in 1662. The ordinary English people quickly followed suit, and before long to them afternoon tea had become a part of their lifestyle. Tea was introduced to Russia by the Kazak people as early as in 1567. The tea trade between China and Russia reached its historic peak in the mid-19th century.

A trading ship owned by the Dutch East India Company moored at Guangzhou Harbor in 1655.

Tea canisters, produced by the British firm of Harney & Sons, bearing the portrait of Queen Catherine, who brought the foreign tea-drinking tradition to England.

103

Russian tea bricks.

A sampler at a British tea company tasting tea leaves.

Liu Junzhou's former residence in Georgia. In the late 19th century, a certain Popov, a Russian merchant, invited Liu and a dozen other Chinese tea workers to Russia to teach him and his fellow countrymen tea growing and processing techniques. In order to commemorate their contributions, the former Soviet government reconstructed Liu's residence in Georgia as a tea museum.

A camel caravan carrying tea to Russia through Zhangjiakou, Hebei Province. Having been purchased and processed by Shanxi Province merchants, tea was transported to Fancheng through Hankou, both in Hubei Province, and on to Zhangjiakou and Guihua (today's Hohhot, Inner Mongolia) through Henan and Shanxi provinces. The caravans would then cross the Gobi Desert and finally reach Kyakhta.

An American trading vessel, the *S.S. Chinese Queen*, arrived in Guangzhou, Guangdong Province, in 1784, and returned with a full load of tea. The tea trade between China and the United States entered an era of high prosperity after that. Seeds of tea plants were introduced into Brazil and Argentina, and cultivated there, in the earlier part of the 19th century.

"The Boston Tea Party." In 1773, a group of citizens boarded three British ships in Boston Harbor, and dumped their cargoes of tea into the sea. This incident is regarded as the spark for the American War of Independence. The protest was against taxation imposed by the British Parliament, including a tax on tea (three pence a pound) imported from China.

A painting showing Chinese tea farmers working on a plantation in Rio de Janeiro, Brazil, done in 1825.

Bibliography

China National Tea Museum, ed., *Savoring Tea and Talking About Tea*, Zhejiang People's Publishing House, 1999.

Wang Congren, *Tea Culture in China*, Shanghai Classics Publishing House, 2001.

Zhao Ziqiang, ed., *Tea Wares of Different Chinese Dynasties*, Guangxi Fine Arts Publishing House, 1999.

Feng Xuemin, *The Homeland of Pu'er Tea*, photo album, Shanghai Calligraphy and Painting Publishing House, 2002.

China Tea Co., Ltd. & China Tea Fans Association, ed., *Chinese Tea over the Past Five Thousand Years*, People's Publishing House, 2001.

Chinese National Geography, September 2002 and December 2002.

Patricia Buckley Ebrey, *The Cambridge Illustrated History of China*. Chinese version by Zhao Shiyu et al., Shandong Pictorial Publishing House, 2001.

China National Native Produce and Animal By-products Import and Export Corporation, ed., *China — The Homeland of Tea*, Hong Kong Culture and Education Publishing House.

William H. Ukers, *All About Tea.*

Huang Shijian & Sha Jin, ed., *A Tableau of the 360 Grassroots Trades in 19th-Century China*, Shanghai Classics Publishing House, 1999.

图书在版编目（CIP）数据

中国茶艺/郭丹英，王建荣编著.
—北京：外文出版社，2003.9
ISBN 978-7-119-03322-8
I. 中... II. ①郭...②王... Ⅲ. 茶－文化－中国－英文
IV.TS971

中国版本图书馆CIP数据核字（2003）第031412号

责任编辑　胡开敏　雷喜红　蔡莉莉
英文翻译　季凯予　郁　苓
英文审核　Paul White　梁良兴
装帧设计　蔡　荣
印刷监制　张国祥

中国茶艺

郭丹英　王建荣 编著

© 外文出版社
出版发行：
外文出版社（中国北京百万庄大街24号）
邮政编码：100037
网址：http://www.flp.com.cn
电话：008610-68320579（总编室）
　　　008610-68995852（发行部）
　　　008610-68327750（版权部）
制版：
外文出版社照排中心
印刷：
北京外文印刷厂
开本：787mm×1092mm　1/20　印张：6
2007年第1版第1次印刷
2009年7月第1版第2次印刷
（英）
ISBN 978-7-119-03322-8
05800（平）
85-E-560P

A giant wild tea tree in Qianjiazhai, Zhenyuan County, Yunnan Province.

Contents

Introduction

China is the birthplace of tea, and the earliest civilization to discover and make use of the plant. The tea plant originated in southwestern China, where the warm and humid climate is very favorable for its growth. Today, people can still find in the area tall *camellia sinensis* trees growing in the wild.

Tea has been an indispensible part of the Chinese people's lives since ancient times. Lin Yutang (1895-1976), a contemporary leading Chinese writer, once wrote, "Chinese people enjoy tea best. They have tea at home, at teahouses, at meetings, at bitter quarrels, or at midnight; with a single pot of tea and nothing else, they can enjoy themselves on any occasion." Indeed, to the Chinese, savoring tea is actually savoring life.

In recent years, Chinese tea culture has been gaining unprecedented momentum. The number of teahouses and the new-style "tea-art houses" keeps growing, and tea culture research institutes are being established across China. Among them, we must particularly mention the China National Tea Museum, located by the West Lake of Hangzhou, Zhejiang Province, home to the famous Longjing (Dragon Well) Tea. Since it was opened in 1991, the museum has been dedicating itself to promoting Chinese tea culture by means of exhibitions and research works that attempt to delve into the deeper structure of the art.

First Edition 2007

Second Printing 2009

Translators: Catherine Jee, Yu Ling

English editors: Paul White, Liang Liangxing

ISBN 978-7-119-03322-8

© Foreign Languages Press, Beijing, China, 2007

Published by Foreign Languages Press

24 Baiwanzhuang Road, Beijing 100037, China

Distributed by China International Book Trading Corporation

35 Chegongzhuang Xilu, Beijing 100044, China

P.O. Box 399, Beijing, China

Printed in the People's Republic of China

The Art of Tea in China

Guo Danying, Wang Jianrong

FOREIGN LANGUAGES PRESS BEIJING

2010

Judy)....

thinking of you
often .... even
in Asia.

I hope you will
enjoy!

With love
and
Friendship,

Diana